Succeeding beyond your Ability
(A Story on Nehemiah)

Cindy Hallam

All Scriptures are from the King James Version of the Bible.

Copyright ©1999 by Cindy Hallam.
International Copyright Secured.
All Rights Reserved.

Except for brief quotations in reviews or articles, prior written permission from the publisher must be secured to use or reproduce any part of this book.
ISBN #0-9661417-2-5

CONTENTS

Introduction	FOCUS	5
Chapter One	COMPASSION	11
Chapter Two	PRAYER	19
Chapter Three	PREPARATION	29
Chapter Four	STRATEGIES	39
Chapter Five	LEADERSHIP	51
Chapter Six	FAITH	63
Chapter Seven	UNITY	71
Chapter Eight	FINISHING	79
Conclusion	SUCCESS	91

Introduction

Focus

Let us rise up and build.
Nehemiah 2:18

What's your latest project that is still unfinished?

Perhaps you're impulsive and plunge right in. Or maybe you're a planner—thinking and talking about what you're going to do—and it takes awhile to get started.

It might be something as mundane as spring-cleaning. Maybe it's painting that spare bedroom, preparing that soon-to-be powerful presentation, reorganizing your garage, writing a book or planting flowers.

Whatever it is, if you are like me, "plunging in" is the easy part. Beginning is fairly simple; like the NIKE advertisements, you "Just Do It!" Practically anyone can get started like a whirlwind.

It's the finishing that's tough!

I don't know how your life is, but I have a trail of things behind me that have gone unfinished. I used to start all kinds of projects. I'd get about halfway through, get tired or bored, and then never finish. I could rationalize it by saying, "Oh, everyone does that," or "I'm gonna do it someday, but I've just got more important things to do right now."

"After all," I've told myself many times, "I could finish it in a jiffy anytime I want to."

It took me awhile to realize that not finishing is a spiritual challenge, not just a physical or mental struggle. I can trace this knowledge to a study of the Old Testament Book of Nehemiah. God began showing me that if I was to be successful in any area of life, I had to finish things stronger than I started. I had to be a "completer," not just a "starter."

As I studied Nehemiah, probably the most astonishing part of what God taught me is that unfinished tasks are very visible indicators of inner character. Half-completed projects weren't harmless "everybody-does-it" trivialities.

Do you remember hearing Aesop's Fable about the rabbit and the turtle? We learned then that the prize doesn't go to the person with the dramatic starting line performance. You have to cross the finish line to win at foot races, building walls and life.

The more I studied Nehemiah, I realized it was more about character building than it was a lesson on teamwork or architecture. Nehemiah set out to rebuild the walls of Jerusalem, and completion was the number one thing on his mind. He was not willing to see it done halfway. He knew that the state of affairs in Jerusalem and the condition of the children of Israel were not the way they should be. These were the people of God, and this was the city of God. Neither should have been in such a miserable state of disarray.

NEHEMIAH THE KING'S CUPBEARER

To set the stage, let's take a quick look at Nehemiah. He lived more than four hundred years before Christ was born. We know that he worked in the Persian palace of King Artaxerxes. Though he was Jewish, Nehemiah held a place of prominence as the King's cupbearer. His job was to taste all food and drink before the king did. It's hard in today's age to

Succeeding beyond your Ability

imagine the vital importance of such a position, but it was a vital position in the King's household. Quoting from German scholar Manfred Barthel's book, *What the Bible Really Says* (William Morrow):

> *In those days when a dose of poison and a bribe for the King's chamberlain were almost invariably the prelude to a coup d'etat, this was a position of the highest trust.*

The phrase "highest trust" implies much. Nehemiah was the last line of defense for poisoned or spoiled food and drink. That seems like a pretty good deal for the king, but I'm not so sure about the cupbearer!

I believe his position implies a very close relationship between Nehemiah and King Artaxerxes. It also tells us some things about Nehemiah's character. There must have been some characteristics about his life that were very strong in order for him to have attained such a high-level position. We can easily assume that he was a person of integrity, that he was trustworthy, and that he had leadership qualities. He wouldn't have been in that position, right below the king, having such a close and trusted relationship with him, without those qualities.

I believe what was on the inside of Nehemiah caused him to begin to desire to rebuild the walls of Jerusalem. Obviously, God knew He could trust him with such a monumental task because God had seen the pattern of his life up until that point. God saw the strengths in his character. He knew that when Nehemiah set out to do something, it was going to happen. And, it wouldn't just be abandoned halfway. The task would be completed.

IMPORTANCE

What significance does this mean for us? After all, what does a rebuilt wall have to do with men and women who live more than twenty centuries later?

What Nehemiah said and did back then relates to everyday issues we face today:

- Work relationships
- Personal and corporate visions
- Discouragement in the midst of challenges
- Criticisms, even from those closest to us
- Perseverance through "impossibilities"
- Finishing strong despite setbacks

Nehemiah is hardly a study of a forgotten civilization. In the pages of the book are timeless and trustworthy strategies that can work as well today as they did for the King's cupbearer.

Says Dr. Charles Swindoll in his timeless book, *Hand Me Another Brick* (Bantam Books):

As you get caught up in the story, you will find yourself engaged in an imaginary dialogue, saying things like, "Nehemiah, you're my kind of guy." I need the characteristics that made you successful transferred into my own life. Hand me another brick, so I might reach my full potential and become all God planned for me to be!

Is that what you want? Do you want to be all God wants you to become? Are you willing to undergo whatever it takes to do what God wants you to do? Most of all, are you willing to let God develop the kind of character inside you that will impact people around you to do great things for Him? Are you willing to let God expand who you are and what you are capable of doing?

If so, the study of Nehemiah can change your life forever, because that's the focus of this book—SUCCEEDING BEYOND YOUR ABILITY.

SUCCESS QUESTIONS

Knowledge is important, but nothing causes change like making knowledge personal. Please take a few moments with each of these questions. Perhaps this would be a good time to start a journal for your answers; when you finish this study of Nehemiah, it can be a great place to see where you have grown.

(1) In terms of not finishing tasks, what areas are weakest for you?

(2) What areas are strongest?

(3) What areas—career, finances, marriage, family, ministry—do you most want to change? Why?

Chapter One

Compassion

Succeeding beyond your Ability

Nehemiah 1: 1-11 is the foundation for SUCCEEDING BEYOND YOUR ABILITY. It centers on the prayer that Nehemiah prayed:

> The words of Nehemiah the son of Hachaliah. And it came to pass in the month Chisleu, in the twentieth year, as I was in Shushan the palace,
>
> That Hanani, one of my brethren, came, he and certain men of Judah; and I asked them concerning the Jews that had escaped, which were left of the captivity, and concerning Jerusalem.
>
> And they said unto me, the remnant that are left of the captivity there in the province are in great affliction and reproach: the wall of Jerusalem also is broken down, and the gates thereof are burned with fire.
>
> Remember, I beseech thee, the word that thou commandedst thy servant Moses, saying, if ye transgress, I will scatter you abroad among the nations:
>
> But if ye turn unto me, and keep my commandments, and do them; though there were of you cast out unto the uttermost part of the heaven, yet will I gather them from thence, and will bring them unto the place that I have chosen to set my name there.
>
> Now these are thy servants and thy people, whom thou hast redeemed by thy great power, and by thy strong hand.
>
> O Lord, I beseech thee, let now thine ear be attentive to the prayer of thy servant, and to the prayer of thy servants, who desire to fear thy name: and prosper, I pray thee, thy servant this day, and grant him mercy in the sight of this man. For I was the King's cupbearer.

RUINS

A bit of history: King Solomon's kingdom had been divided between Israel (the northern tribes) and Judah (the southern tribes). Because of continued disobedience, Israel was taken into captivity and King Nebuchadnezzar invaded Jerusalem and all Judah and took the people captive.

As God's people were allowed to return to their land (recorded in the Book of Ezra), reports of the devastation filtered back to those still in captivity. Nehemiah lived in Susa, the capital of the Medio-Persian Empire, the favorite winter residence of the Persian kings.

Nehemiah, according to the first century historian Josephus, overheard people conversing in the Hebrew language. These travelers had returned of late from Judea. Nehemiah eagerly inquired about the homeland of his ancestors. What he heard must have been overwhelming—the unfinished and desolate condition of Jerusalem, as well as the downtrodden and defenseless state of the exiles who had returned. The temple and some private dwellings had been rebuilt, but the walls and gates of the city had been allowed to remain a mass of shattered ruins, dating back to the Chaldean wars.

The children of God and the city of Jerusalem were constantly in Nehemiah's heart and on his mind. They were very precious to him. Even though he could not see them, he had not forgotten about them. There was a concern in his life for the children of God, so he asked about their welfare.

In verse 2 we find: *One of my brethren, came, he and certain men of Judah; and I asked them concerning the Jews that had escaped, which were left of the captivity, and concerning Jerusalem.*

The fact that his inquiry is mentioned here gives us the impression that it was the very first thing he asked these men.

In verse 3 he writes: *And they said unto me, The remnant that are left of the captivity there in the province are in great affliction and reproach: the wall of Jerusalem also is broken down, and gates thereof are burned with fire.*

Now, if you got a report like that about your family and your relatives you would probably be upset and distressed too. Even though what Nehemiah heard was not what he wanted to hear, it may have not come as a great surprise because of what had been taking place in the lives of the children of Israel up to this point. They had been in captivity, they had escaped, and then they had gone back to Jerusalem. As mentioned earlier, the temple had been rebuilt, but the walls were not. There was a partial restoration that had taken place, but it had never been completed.

GOD'S DESIRE

Have you ever noticed that God always completes what He begins? When He restores something, He desires to restore it completely.

When Nehemiah heard that the walls were broken down and the gates were burned with fire, he knew that what he heard was not the plan of God. That seems to be what exploded in his spirit. God doesn't do things halfway! Ezra had done a partial restoration of the temple, but it hadn't been completed. Nehemiah was not content to sit back and to see the walls and the people of Israel remain in that state.

Some of the commentaries and research available on this subject will tell you that the people were not living within the city because there was no wall or enclosure around the city. This further implies that they were not where they were supposed to be. Although they were not in as bad of a state as the pagan people of that area, they were still living among people that didn't serve God.

God had called His children out. He had called them to separate themselves from evil influences. Because of the state of affairs of the city of Jerusalem, the children of Israel were still able to filter back out and intermingle with other people. They were where they shouldn't have been.

Now when we think about our society today, we know that we can go easily from one city to the next. We don't have to go through a huge gate, nor do we have to stop and ask if we can have permission to enter into the city. Things are pretty much open to us today, but it wasn't that way in Nehemiah's time. The purpose of the city wall was for protection. It was designed to guard the people of God from the influence of those who were outside of the city. It not only protected them from being harmed physically, but it also protected them emotionally and spiritually. God had called his children to be separated, but the wall was broken down. There was nothing to protect God's children.

When Nehemiah heard this, verse 4, he responded to the news: *And it came to pass, when I heard these words, that I sat down and wept, and mourned certain days, and fasted, and prayed before the God of heaven.*

He heard what was taking place in their lives. They were close to his heart. He cared for these people. The news motivated him to respond and that response was one of weeping, prayer and fasting. He had compassion for his people!

IMPACT

You can't watch or listen to the evening news without hearing about horrible things that are going on in the world around us—the latest crime statistics, another bloody Third World coup, a kidnapping in a neighboring town, gunfire in streets and schools. What we hear may upset us or even make us sorrowful, but are we ever moved to the degree that we actually do anything about it?

Nehemiah's heart was grieved for his people. However, what he did changed history. What we learn from his actions can change us forever, too!

SUCCESS QUESTIONS

(1) What kind of a person, from what you've read, was Nehemiah?
(2) What traits did he have that you share?
(3) How was he different from you?
(4) What most recently touched you to the point of compassion?
(5) In the past, what have you done to change the things which touch you that deeply?

Chapter Two

Prayer

*And it came to pass, when I heard these words, that I
sat down and wept, and mourned certain days, and
fasted, and prayed before
the God of heaven.
Nehemiah 1:4*

Nehemiah had true, heart-felt compassion. This wasn't a "I-feel-your-pain-but-don't-know-what-to-do-about-it" sympathy. The King's cupbearer's compassion moved him to weep and mourn. It didn't stop there. He fasted and prayed before the God of heaven. He took the emotional feeling of knowing what Israel was going through, then went one step further. He began to fast and pray concerning the needs of the people. I believe this is a pattern for us to study.

INTERCESSION

One of the best ways to know God's direction is when we feel a special, deep need to pray. Why? God wants to use us as intercessors—as people who see the needs of others. More importantly, He wants us to do something about that need.

We must recognize that when the compassion of God is stirred on the inside of us, we have to take it a step further by fasting and praying about those things. In some situations, we can actually go and physically do something to be of assistance. But we know that a great majority of situations are not like that.

God wants to draw us to the place that when He speaks to us concerning a situation, He knows we're going to take that into a time of prayer. He desires for us to be a people who will intercede for the needs of other people.

Maybe you're thinking about times in the past when God has spoken to your heart about something you've seen or heard, and maybe you've been moved to tears over some of those things. Yet you did nothing about it. Understand that there are times when God speaks to your heart, but He's not just looking for your compassion. He wants you to lift your voice in prayer on behalf of whatever that need may be.

Nehemiah's earnest and protracted prayer reflects a deeply patriotic man who seemingly felt that his life would be changed forever by the events ahead of him.

PRAYER AND FASTING

Sensing the urgency of the need back in Jerusalem, Nehemiah didn't just pray. He prayed and he fasted. Fasting to you and me generally means that we feel led to give up food or maybe a particular food item for a certain amount of time. However, the real motive of fasting is that we are willing to deprive ourselves of something that we enjoy in order to pray for the needs of someone else.

This happened to me just recently while I was working on this study. I was getting dressed. It was a particularly busy morning, but I suddenly felt the Holy Spirit nudging me to pray for a specific need within the ministry. This isn't unusual, since Abundant Life Christian Center has grown so much and many needs are represented. We not only have thousands of people who are part of the church, but we have numerous local, national and international outreaches that are part of this ministry. So I started praying. Ten seconds hadn't passed when something else popped into my mind. My mind was instantly diverted. I wasn't praying anymore, I was just thinking about whatever else had popped into my mind. So, I thought to myself, " I'm going to get refocused here and pray." Well, it wasn't ten seconds before the same thing happened again. To me, it was a signal that I needed to completely get rid of all other thoughts and focus on what God was trying to tell me. That led to a time of fasting, especially after the Lord showed me areas within the ministry that had specific, urgent needs.

There are times that we just have to stop what we're doing and focus on prayer. It isn't easy, but when it gets cloudy, it is especially important to fast as you pray.

DISCIPLINE

We generally can't pray and do something else at the same time. Certainly it's hard to do both effectively. We can drive down the road and pray in the Holy Ghost; that's always a good thing. But there are those times when God calls us aside. He says, "Stop everything else you're doing. I want you to go into a time of prayer." In order to do that, it often means that we must deprive or discipline ourselves.

What do you give up? It might be something that you wanted to do—an activity or purchase. It can be something that you enjoy—meals or a specific food. It has to be personal for you. You need to seek God for what you should fast. It probably won't be anything drastic.

It's a time you can say, "I was going to watch a television program, but I won't do that. Instead, I'll turn it off and go and pray until You show me or I believe I've prayed it through."

Fasting often involves giving up food at times, and that's the common association we have with that term. But we can choose to give up anything. It's a matter of giving up something and putting ourselves aside in order to pray for the needs that we see are evident in the lives of other people.

All of us know people who need our prayers. Even a very general prayer can work. You may say, "God, I know your Word never returns to You void and that prayer always works." This is certainly the mercy and grace of God at work. God does answer prayer. But for real results, you may be required to be a little more diligent in your prayers—committed prayers that may demand fasting, as well.

DILIGENCE

I believe we should look carefully at Nehemiah's zeal as a prayer warrior. He didn't pray for five minutes. The Bible points to him weeping and mourning for days as he fasted and prayed before God. The miserable and weak state of the children of Israel and the city of Jerusalem was something quite serious to him.

We need to come to the place in our lives where we take seriously what is going on in the lives of people in our church, schools, cities and in our world. What a change it would make if more people would begin praying earnestly for our communities and nations.

God actually promised to affect entire societies when His people pray diligently: *If my people, which are called by my name, shall humble themselves, and pray, and seek my face, and turn from their wicked ways; then will I hear from heaven, and will forgive their sin, and will heal their land. (2 Chronicles 7:14)*

Right after He taught about mustard seed faith, Jesus said that nothing was impossible to those who understand the value of diligent prayer: *Howbeit this kind goeth not out but by prayer and fasting. (Matthew 17:21)*

Many times it only takes you to make a difference. It requires that you spend time fasting and praying over a need. God can and does meet the needs of people based upon the prayers of one individual. How much more powerful could it be then if more than one person would take it seriously and pray? What could God do if we were in unity, praying over the needs that we see around us?

Many times people spend an enormous amount of time talking about a problem, or time discussing what should happen now, how it ought to be, and why it's the way it is. The time could usually be better spent praying, instead of all the discussion.

Nehemiah didn't spend a lot of time going into all the details with the people who came back from Jerusalem. He heard the report, it grieved his spirit and he went into a time of prayer. Many times if we don't act when the Holy Ghost speaks to our hearts, we override that prompting. We can override the feeling of compassion that may be birthed by the Word of God. Too often we wait too long until that feeling of a necessity to pray has passed.

I wonder what would have happened if Nehemiah had let that stirring pass? What if he had not felt the necessity and moved on it immediately?

"Oh, I'll pray later."

Most of us know that "later" never comes. We forget the commitment that we've made. Don't override a time of prayer when God speaks. Move with that prompting and act quickly.

PRAYER POINTS

In Nehemiah's prayer we see some powerful elements.
- He acknowledged the position that God held in his life.
- He called himself a servant of God.
- He *declared* that he knew God would meet his need.
- He had *confidence* that God would meet his need.
- He *believed* that God would meet his need and the needs of his people.

Succeeding beyond your Ability

Armed with powerful prayer, Nehemiah believed he was going to go to Jerusalem where the wall was going to be rebuilt and the place of protection that God had established for His people would be restored. The compassion of his heart toward the people of God is clearly seen. And we're going to see that his actions produced great results.

The desire of Nehemiah should also be our desire. We must seek that level of compassion. We must believe that God will work life-changing miracles in the lives of people around us. Most importantly, we must pray effectively and thereby see results produced.

It's time that we realized what the Bible has sought to teach we are to be salt and light. We are to be change-agents by taking the Gospel from door to door and shore to shore. We must impact our generation and therefore influence generations to come. To do less should be unthinkable.

SUCCESS QUESTIONS

As with Nehemiah, all of our dreams and visions must be tied into God's overall plan. It wasn't the condition of Jerusalem's walls that saddened Nehemiah and caused him to begin praying and fasting. It was the spiritual devastation of the children of Israel that moved him with compassion. It was the bigger picture!

As you seek to see God's direction in your life, spend time meditating on these questions:

(1) Of all the dreams you've had for your life, what ONE thing would you most like to come true?

(2) What has kept that dream from happening?

(3) What action steps would you put together if you knew, beyond any doubt, that you could not fail in reaching your dream?

Chapter Three

Preparation

Succeeding beyond your Ability

Nehemiah was moved with compassion for the children of Israel and the destruction of Jerusalem, but he was faced with several details that made rebuilding the walls highly improbable—at least in the natural realm. For starters, he lived 800 miles from the problem. Next, he held a ranking position with one of the world's most powerful kings. Quite honestly, why would King Artaxerxes allow his trusted cupbearer to leave for an undetermined period of time to lead a team in a relatively unimportant village?

GROUNDWORK

So Nehemiah prayed and fasted. One of the greatest, most obvious needs was for God to touch the King's heart. However, instead of marching into the King's presence and demanding time off, royal transportation and numerous resources, Nehemiah sought God's will. What happened was nothing short of miraculous.

> *And it came to pass in the month Nissan, in the twentieth year of Artaxerxes the king, that wine was before him: and I took up the wine, and gave it unto the king. Now I had not been before time sad in his presence.*
> *Wherefore the king said unto me, Why is thy countenance sad, seeing thou art not sick? This is nothing else but sorrow of heart. Then I was very sore afraid. (Nehemiah 2:1-2)*

Actually, I don't believe that Nehemiah was afraid in the way that you and I might have been afraid. His fear was directly related to the enormous amount of respect that he had for the king. He may have been a little apprehensive, but things were already settled in his heart. He had asked God for favor and mercy with the king in advance. So when he went to make his petition known, Nehemiah believed that he was going to get what he wanted. There was a confidence in his heart that God was going to see him through. After all, the desire of his heart was also the desire of God's heart. It involved the people of God.

CHARACTER

The king saw something different about Nehemiah. His cupbearer had never before been sad in his presence. The king had to ask him why he was downhearted.

The fact that Nehemiah had never appeared to be depressed before is amazing. Please remember that we are talking about a man who was in captivity. He wasn't with his own people. He wasn't in his own city. Yet, even though he was with the king on a daily basis, never had King Artaxerxes detected sadness or sorrow in Nehemiah's life.

That's a powerful statement concerning his character. He had remained steadfast and confident, sure of his position and his walk with God. Up to this point in time, he had not allowed the circumstances to change his countenance. And even though his appearance may have momentarily changed, his faith was unwavering. That's a strong position.

The king knew immediately that something was wrong. He knew that there was something troubling Nehemiah because he saw it in his countenance. His countenance also revealed the extent of his desire toward the people of God. Nehemiah had heard a negative report and it troubled him greatly. The concern in his inner man was evident by his outward appearance. It is apparent that under normal day-to-day situations, he was able to control himself to the degree that his emotions didn't get the best of him. But this was not a normal situation. These were God's people. This was the city of God. It concerned a place that was supposed to be a refuge and a place of protection for the people of God.

Sometimes we get so wrapped up in our own little everyday problems of life that everybody around us knows the moment we stub our toe. They can look at us and know immediately we've either had a confrontation with our kids, a fight with our spouse or that the bills aren't getting paid. They can tell by our countenance when anything is wrong. In the light of the issues of the kingdom, what importance do those things really have?

Now, I know God wants us blessed, and He wants all those things to turn out in our favor, but often we have to walk through them to get on the other side to that victory. I'm sure that Nehemiah probably encountered monumental challenges every day. Think about it—he went to work every day knowing that he was just one mouthful of poison away from death. That could be a pretty depressing position, so he probably had bad days occasionally.

Yet the Word says the king had never seen him with a sad look on his face. He had reached a place, even in captivity, where he was able to control his emotions. Faced with death daily, he could still let the peace of God shine through him. The opposite of sorrow is joy, and since the king had never seen Nehemiah sorrowful, the joy of the Lord was obviously evident in his life.

Granted, Nehemiah wasn't doing what he wanted to do, even though he had one of the best positions that a man in captivity could have. I'm sure he would have much preferred to be with his own people and in his own city, not in a place where he had to ask the King's permission for everything he did.

So, Nehemiah was in a place where, given the opportunity, he would have chosen somewhere else to be and something else to do. Have you ever found yourself in that situation before? You would choose something else or someplace else if it were left up to you. But even during times when our emotions and situations try to be in control, we've got to rise above those emotions and build ourselves up in the spirit. We need to stand strong in God. We need to let the Holy Ghost produce a strength inside us so that those situations in life do not control us.

How many times are we controlled in the course of a day, rather than being in control? We can lose days sometimes because of one minor little problem. Everyone with whom we come in contact knows we've got a problem. Sometimes we even get to the place where we find pleasure in the fact that other people know we're going through a difficult time. It becomes a sympathy and a victim-type thing. Face it, we all like people to know that it's really rough. Not Nehemiah—this was a first for him.

The only thing Nehemiah let anyone know about was his great compassion for the people and city of God. He got to the place in his conflict that it didn't have anything to do with him, but it had everything to do with the well-being of other people.

That should inspire us to set our sights a little higher than the daily routine in life. If I asked you to take out a piece of paper and make a list of 15 or 20 things that you would change if you had the choice, it wouldn't take you any time at all. We would all love to give that list to God and ask Him to change everything that seems bad or unpleasant. But how important are those things?

Nehemiah didn't just get upset about the whole thing and walk around with a sad countenance. The Bible says that he prayed and fasted. He was willing to give up his time, energy and effort in order to pray for the people of God. But that wasn't enough. He was even willing to give up his place of comfort in order to help God's people.

Preparation

King Artaxerxes asked, "What's wrong? Why is sorrow in your heart?" At that point Nehemiah had a choice to make. He either had to speak the truth and reveal his true feelings, or he had to cover up what was stirring in his heart.

How often do we find ourselves in the place where we have to make a similar decision? Do we risk speaking the truth and reveal what God has spoken to us, or do we just cover it up?

Nehemiah's countenance has prompted the king to ask him what was wrong. Notice his response in verse 3: *Let the king live forever: why should not my countenance be sad, when the city, the place of my fathers' sepulcers, lieth waste, and the gates thereof are consumed with fire?*

The king responded by asking his cupbearer, "What do you want?"

That is an amazing question. Can't you see the favor of God working through this? For the king to have noticed a servant's countenance, to ask him about his state of mind, and to be concerned about his well-being was miraculous. Beyond that, the king responded by asking Nehemiah what he could do for him.

Now, realistically, how many servants would normally get to place their requests before the king? It is not hard to imagine that this was a very rare occurrence. As servants of God, you and I have free access to place our requests before God at any time, but that wasn't true in the king and servant relationship, however intimate and trusting. Yet the king re-

Succeeding beyond your Ability

sponded favorably to his cupbearer.

In verse 5, Nehemiah responded to the king: *If it pleased the king and if thy servant has found favor in thy sight, that thou would ascend me to Judah to the city of my father's sepulcher that I may build it. And the king said unto me, the queen also sitting by him, For how long shall thy journey be and when will thou return?*

I wonder what Nehemiah was thinking. First of all the king had said, "My, you look sad today, Nehemiah. I have never seen you look like this before. What's wrong?" Nehemiah had responded by describing the state of a desolate city 800 miles away. In the natural, the king didn't have a keen interest in Jerusalem or the people of God. Yet his response was very favorable and indicated a willingness to let his trusted confidante go.

Nehemiah saw that God had opened the door. Likewise, we need to have the eye of the spirit. We need to see when God opens up those doors for us. We miss so many opportunities because we see with natural eyes. We pay more attention to feelings and emotions, then we miss when God opens up mighty doors.

Nehemiah recognized that this was one of those doors. He said, "This is what I want to do—I want to go and I want to rebuild the city of God."

How stupid does that sound? Nehemiah is one man. He is a cupbearer in the King's palace. Yet he tells the king, "I want to go and rebuild the walls around the city of Jerusalem." In the natural, without God, that king probably would have laughed in his face.

It could have been much like the response young David received when he announced that he would face Goliath. I can hear Jesse's sons mocking, "David, what are you doing here? This is the battlefront. This is a major-league giant. You are not trained. You're just a shepherd boy. What are you doing here, David? Go back home and feed your sheep."

But David didn't do what the people around him said. He saw the opportunity. He saw himself in the eyes of God. He said, "God has won victories for me before, and God is going to do it again."

Nehemiah wasn't moved by the fact that he was only one man. He knew there were people in Jerusalem whom he could rally together. He looked forward to encouraging the people of the Lord. He had been praying over them. He knew God was going to meet his need.

Prayer and fasting had been Nehemiah's first step. When the door opened for him, it was *supernaturally natural* to proclaim boldly and confidently, "I want to go and rebuild the walls around the city of God."

The king didn't laugh at him. The king didn't say, "You must be crazy! You're a captive. What makes you think I am going to let you go?" Instead, he asked how long he needed to be gone. Then the king gave him a commission as deputy governor of Judea, accompanied by a military guard and invested with full power to obtain materials for rebuilding the wall. How much better does it get?

Succeeding beyond your Ability

The God-breathed, patriotic wish of Nehemiah's heart was honored. Life for the cupbearer and the children of Israel was about to change beyond their wildest dreams. They were to be instruments of change to revive the city of Jerusalem to the ancient glory of their forefathers!

SUCCESS QUESTIONS

(1) Preparation through prayer and fasting is one of the great Biblical keys to success. What adjustments could you make to become more diligent at prayer and fasting?

(2) What changes are you willing to make in order to become more successful in different areas of your life?

Chapter Four

Strategies

Can you imagine what passed through Nehemiah's mind when King Artaxerxes gave him *carte blanche* to return to Jerusalem and rebuild the walls? My heart would have been beating so hard in my chest anyone could have heard it. The normal person would be jumping up and down, perhaps doing cartwheels. Not Nehemiah. He was already putting together strategies to rebuild the walls. He was also showing the character traits of a trusted servant.

TRUTHFULNESS

We read in verse 6 of Chapter 2: *So it pleased the king to send me and I set him a time.*

Nehemiah got to choose how long he wanted to be gone! He was given permission to tell the king what he wanted to do, how long it was going to take, and what he was going to need to accomplish the task. And then Nehemiah gave a definite time when he would return to resume his position as cupbearer.

Nehemiah walked in boldness and assertiveness that had been established in his heart by prayer. He walked out the confidence that had been established by prayer in his heart. Then he saw God move in a mighty way.

The end of verse 8 reveals: *And the king granted me according to the good hand of my God upon me.*

Nehemiah didn't take credit for what happened. When he got to Jerusalem and began to talk to the people, he didn't say, "Hey, let me tell you my story. I was in such a good position with the king. I was his cupbearer. I was his loyal, trustworthy servant. I got to taste all his wine and food before he ever tasted it. He liked me so much that he gave me everything I asked for. He let me come here to rebuild the city."

No, he didn't say any of those things. Instead, he told the people of Jerusalem that the king granted his requests because of the hand of God that was upon him. He acknowledged that it was God working on his behalf.

You know, we take too much credit sometimes. We think, "Man, I must have really done a good job. You know, they really like me." It has nothing to do with you. It has everything to do with the power of God working in you.

We need to remember when we pray that God is going to move, not because of who we are, but because of who God is. When we're walking in the ways of God, desiring to do his will, God is going to move on our behalf.

PREPARATION

Nehemiah was naturally guarded about his commission. We read in verse 11 and 12: *I came to Jerusalem and I was there three days. I rose in the night. I and some few men with me neither told any man what my God had put in my heart to do at Jerusalem.*

So far the only person with whom he shared details of his plan was King Artaxerxes. When he arrived in the city of Jerusalem, he took time to do research and to prepare. Too many times it is so easy to open our mouths too soon, but Nehemiah was different.

Nehemiah knew he would have to stand in the position as a leader among a people who had been in distress, who had been discouraged and who had been run out of their city by the people around them. He saw the necessity of coming up with a good plan. First he would need to have a confidence in his heart about what he was going to do or the people wouldn't follow him.

You and I know that we won't follow people who don't know what they're talking about. The people of Nehemiah's day were no different. That's why Nehemiah took the time he needed to observe what had taken place in the city. He didn't share his plan with anyone, nor did he seek another opinion. He slipped out, under the cloak of night, and observed all that had taken place in the city and with the people.

I believe that while Nehemiah was observing the destruction of the city and its walls, God was speaking to his heart. God was giving him the plan that he was to present to the people. It would be a plan that the people could receive and then follow so Nehemiah could lead them and complete the task he had set out to accomplish.

God calls us to be leaders in many different areas. He calls us to be leaders in our homes, local church, communities, in relationship to our children, and on our jobs. *We need well-devised plans in order to function correctly in a leadership role.* Those plans must revolve around the Word of God.

We must also take the time to devise our plans so there is no room for failure. Our plans must revolve around our knowledge of the Word of God. In anything that you hope to accomplish, or for any goal that you set, you need steps to help you reach your goals. If you don't take the time to establish those steps, you may never reach your goal because you have gone into it without knowledge and understanding.

When you take the time necessary to develop your plan of action, you have greater control over your success. God wants us to be successful. He wanted Nehemiah to be successful. Not only did the plan affect Nehemiah's life, but also it affected a whole group of people and a city that God called His own. Nehemiah was wise enough to know that he could not just go in and do it on his own. He hadn't gotten as far as he had by his own ability. It was the hand of God that was upon him. He was favored by God. He observed for three days before he acted. Preparation time is never wasted time.

OBSERVATION

Up to the point where Nehemiah and his troop rode into Jerusalem, the only thing he had to go on was reports from people returning to Persia. He had not seen Jerusalem with his own eyes. He had not witnessed the destruction for himself. Here is a great lesson: Observe for yourself before jumping to conclusions. Seek to make sure that your information is true and correct.

Nehemiah made sure, through firsthand observation, that the reports were true. We all know how many times things get blown out of proportion. Neighborhoods, churches, cities and even nations have been broken up over false or exaggerated information. You show wisdom when you do research to confirm the accuracy of data. You need to be sure that you haven't received reports that are fabricated in some way, blown out of proportion or twisted. You need to make sure that your information is correct before you pursue a solution.

When Nehemiah made his observations and had it all straight in his mind, then he went to the people.

SOLUTIONS

Then said I unto them, you see the distress that we are in, how Jerusalem lies waste and the gates are burned with fire? Come and let us build up the walls of Jerusalem that we be no more a reproach. Then I told them of the hand of my God which was good upon me and also the King's words that he had spoken unto me, and they said, Let us rise up and build. So they strengthened their hands for this good work. (Nehemiah 2:17-18)

Notice that Nehemiah includes himself as being in distress with them. He had experienced firsthand, though on a limited scale, what they had gone through. Now everything he tells them is producing confidence that they can rebuild the walls.

It only seems logical, in light of their circumstances, at least some of the people had a burning desire in their hearts to do something about the state in which they lived. However, for whatever reason, there was no confidence among the people that they could do it. Now Nehemiah appears with a commission in hand and resources to do the job. He tells them, "We're in sad shape, but we can do something about it. God has had mercy on me and I have found favor with the king. Now, let us rise up and build. Let's take action!"

Positive action happens when someone is bold enough to speak the truth, to speak it in confidence, and to say, "Look, God is for you and I'm going to work with you."

Where would you be today if nobody had ever said that to you? At some time or another, every one of us has had somebody come to us and say, "God is for you and I'm going to pray for you. I'm going to be there for you. I'm going to work with you. I'm going to do whatever I can do to help you." That was the beginning place of our confidence to move out of the state we were living in. It brought us out of the place of distress, waste and turmoil. With confidence and faith, you finally began restoring your life and started SUCCEEDING BEYOND YOUR ABILITY.

Succeeding beyond your Ability

Nehemiah knew that. He took the opportunity to speak encouragement to the people around him. In 2:18, the people of Jerusalem replied: *Let us rise up and build. So they strengthened their hands for this good work.*

They joined together in unity. They combined skills and abilities. They realized that they had something important they could do. When they found out they had a leader, they were ready to go to work.

MORE CRITICISM

Professional critics Sanballat and Tobiah were joined by Geshem the Arabian. They heard what was going on and in verse 19: *...they laughed us to scorn and despised us and said, What is this that you do? Will you rebel against the king?*

I find it interesting that the critics accused Nehemiah and the people of Jerusalem of rebelling against the king. Who was rebelling? The king had already given his permission.

You see, the critics told a lie. They tried to get the children of God to believe the lie. However, because Nehemiah knew that he was commissioned by the king they would not believe the lie. The commission proved that the children of Israel weren't rebelling against the king; therefore, the lie of these enemies couldn't shatter Nehemiah's confidence. He was walking in truth. He was walking in integrity. He was walking in obedience to the command of the king. That made all the difference in the world.

When we walk in integrity, when we speak the truth and when we honor God, the lies of the enemy should never shatter our confidence. We need to know where we stand. We must be sure of God's calling. We need to know that our desires are God's desires.

Then, when enemies and critics try to sway us with official-sounding accusations, we can say as Nehemiah confessed: *Then answered I them, and said unto them: The God of Heaven, he will prosper us. Therefore, we, his servants, will arise and build, but you have no portion nor right nor memorial in Jerusalem. (Nehemiah 2:20)*

We have to make a decision when people laugh at us, ridicule us or tell us something that is contrary to the ways of God. That decision must be to stand firm in our commission. We cannot let lies discourage us from the work of God. We must have enough so that no incorrect data or false accusation of the enemy can cause us to turn aside.

BEYOND CRITICISM

We must recognize that the first criticism by poorly-intentioned neighbors was not the end of Nehemiah's obstacles. It was just the beginning. By this time, however, nothing else mattered but the vision of rebuilding the walls.

I believe Nehemiah said to himself, "You know, I've gotten this far and I'm not about to turn back now. You can laugh or do whatever you want to do. I am here by a command of the king. I am here because you are God's people and this is

God's city and I am going to do what I said I was going to do. Not only that, but I've got people gathered around me who are willing to work and finish the task."

As Nehemiah knew, we are never alone when it comes to God's work. It takes determination to rise to a position of a leader, to know that we stand in the power and in the anointing of God, and to know that God is on our side. When we reach that place, we can truly reach far beyond our own abilities. We can realize that God has supernatural resources—time, money, people, plans—available for us.

Don't ever let critics discourage you. You must recognize the truth that wells up in your heart. You must understand the power available to you. After all, God can do anything. He can restore. He can rebuild. He can gather together. He can strengthen. He can give supernatural resources. He can do whatever He wants. That is the desire of His heart.

Preparation is the key! God's strategies, based on preparation, can change lives forever.

SUCCESS QUESTIONS

(1) From what you've seen thus far, what ONE quality from Nehemiah's life would you like to make stronger in your own life?

(2) Nehemiah believed that God would give his team success ("God will prosper us!"). Do you feel comfortable with God and success in the same sentence? Why or why not?

(3) In your own words, how does God's concept of success differ from the world's concept?

(4) What does success mean to you?

Chapter Five

Leadership

So far we've seen some outstanding character traits in Nehemiah's life. These characteristics promoted him as a leader. As we look at his life, we can learn how we are to respond in any place of leadership to which God calls.

Some readers may say, "But I'm not really a leader. I'm not the head of a corporation, church, or organization."

If you are alive, you are either a leader or a leader-in-training. You are a leader in your home, job or church. God can even place you in the position of a leader among your circle of friends. You can be the person to whom people look when they're seeking the counsel of God.

"These are the hard times in which a genius would wish to live," said Abigail Adams, wife of the second United States' President and mother of the nation's sixth President. She then added: "Great necessities call forth great leaders."

Now, more than ever, we need people who have the character and anointing to be great leaders in all areas of society. Are you ready?

CHARACTER

There are several absolute necessities for those who would be leaders. Up to this point, we've seen that Nehemiah, one of his generation's great leaders, had these character traits:

- ♦ Compassion
- ♦ A commitment to prayer and fasting
- ♦ Preparation and organization
- ♦ Boldness

Wouldn't you like to see these traits increase in your life? Nehemiah knew he wouldn't be able to tackle a task of this size without these character strengths. There was a big job to be done. Big people (in character, not necessarily size) had to step forward.

THE NEED

If you've ever done any remodeling in your home, you know what a tremendous task that is. I remember one time we added on a room to our house. It was just one room and seemed as if it would be relatively simple. Wrong! I thought we would never get it finished. There was dust and debris everywhere. This went on for what seemed like an eternity. It was just horrible. The end result was wonderful, but the process was not very fun—especially toward the end. What helped Walter and me to press on and not get overwhelmed was the promise of the end result. We made a plan. We worked that plan, knowing what the final outcome would be.

Back to Nehemiah—let's recap. He knew in order for the people of God to have the place of refuge God desired, he was going to have to go and help rebuild the city. When the cupbearer arrived in Jerusalem, he confirmed that the walls were broken down and the gates had been burned with fire. Worse, the people of God were scattered. They weren't living inside the city because the protective wall was ruined.

From a human perspective, I can only imagine what he thought as he surveyed the situation. On the one hand, he must have wondered, "How are we going to get this job done?" On the other, he had to be excited at the idea seeing such a wonderful vision come together. Remember, Nehemiah had been a captive in a faraway land. After a lifetime of menial tasks, he must have felt a remarkable feeling of freedom and excitement at rebuilding the wall around the great city of God. If he had discouraging thoughts, Nehemiah overcame them as he pressed on to do what he knew God had called him to do.

I don't know about you, but there have been many times in my life when God has spoken something to me, and the very first thing I thought was, "God, I can't do that. It's simply too much for me. I don't have what it takes." That's not the response God wants from us. We must never lose sight of the fact that God never calls us to do anything in our own strength or based on our own ability. He calls us to work in His strength and His anointing. If He calls us to do something, then He always provides everything we need to get the job done. He desires that we succeed beyond our abilities.

ORGANIZATION

Nehemiah looked at the tremendous task that was in front of him and said, "If this is going to work, we have to have organization. We have to have cooperation." In the last three verses of Chapter 2, Nehemiah assembled the elders, produced his commission from King Artaxerxes and exhorted the people of Jerusalem to assist in the work. Their spirits were revived, and the children of Israel decided to commit to the work, despite the taunts from Sanballat, Tobiah and Geshem.

Now, look at verses 1 through 3 of Chapter 3: *Then Eliashib the high priest rose up with his brethren the priests, and they builded the sheep gate; they sanctified it, and set up the doors of it; even unto the tower of Meah they sanctified it, unto the tower of Hananeel. And next unto him builded the men of Jericho. And next to them builded Zaccur the son of Imri. But the fish gate did the sons of Hassenaah build, who also laid the beams thereof, and set up the doors thereof, the locks thereof, and the bars thereof.*

So it goes on throughout Chapter 3—name after name, group after group. Every segment of Jerusalem's society was organized to have a part in what was taking place, from the priests to the everyday workers. Under Nehemiah's leadership, the wall was divided into segments, one of which was assigned respectively to each of the leading families who had returned from captivity to Jerusalem.

Granted, Nehemiah was the leader. He could have gone in, cleared everybody out and said, "God spoke to me to come and rebuild the city of Jerusalem. Now, I want everybody to get out of the way and I'm going to do it." Had he approached the task in that manner, probably the task would have never been completed. No one man can accomplish the work of God alone.

Succeeding beyond your Ability

Nehemiah knew that the people were vital in order for the rebuilding effort to be successful, so he began to designate who was going to build or repair each portion. When you read commentaries and studies about Nehemiah, you will find that each of these groups were actually building in a place that was very close to their own place of residence. He didn't take one family or group from over here and say go way over there and build something. He made it as comfortable and convenient as possible for each person to be involved in this project. This resulted in great cooperation among the people as they set out to do the work of God.

We don't know exactly how many people participated in the project. When one man's name is mentioned, a group of people are represented those workers associated with a particular segment of the wall. It is easy to assume that thousands of people worked to rebuild the walls and the gates of Jerusalem. With that many people, cooperation was a necessity. There was little room for strife or jealousy. No where is it recorded that anyone said, "Hey, that's my job. You get away from that. Don't do that. Stand back and let me do that because I have more skill than you."

For the rebuilding to happen in 52 days, the people had to be willing to work together, as unto the Lord.

Doesn't God require the same commitment today?

TEAMWORK

Can you get a visual picture of these thousands of men and women working in this capacity? They were all next to each other rebuilding the walls, so the people of God would be blessed and protected. They probably worked long hours and long days. It wasn't work like you and I know in the 21st century. It was work that didn't stop at 4:30 in the afternoon!

They were willing to work together and to cooperate with one another to ensure it got accomplished. Through Nehemiah's plan and organization, these people focused on their specific tasks.

Nothing works without a plan—or without teamwork. Nehemiah's plan kept people focused on their task. He was obviously specific. His plan broke a very big job down into smaller tasks that weren't overwhelming. If you are overwhelmed, then your tendency may be to just sit back, stare and think about everything that needs to be done. You probably won't get to the actual work because it seems too big. Through his planning and organization, Nehemiah took everything to a level of possibility to these men and women. They were not overwhelmed.

Sometimes we tend to get a little on the spiritual side when it comes to plans. We step out in faith, hoping everything will fall into place. Surely God has a plan, so why shouldn't we? After all, we don't need to designate to others what they need to be doing since God will undoubtedly speak to them. That happens sometimes.

I think God gets blamed many times for the failures that happen as a result of our own lack of planning and leadership. Certainly, God doesn't remove the need for the natural, practical, planning side of things just because we are spiritual people. We are living in a natural world. We still have to function realistically and naturally, even though God empowers us spiritually.

Nehemiah understood this principle of leadership. He had a plan. He organized the people. He was able to accomplish the miraculous because he functioned wisely in his role as a leader.

In your own leadership role, there are areas where you need planning and organization in order for everything to get done that needs to be done. If you don't do what you need to do, then others will not know what they are supposed to do.

FAMILIES

Through planning and organization we can have orderly lives. That's one of the best ways we train our children. We give them small tasks that gradually develop into larger tasks. We give them a specific plan of action. We tell them, "If you'll do it this way, then this will happen. When you do it this way, this will be easier." Teach your children how to organize and how to plan. Teach them how to break a big project down into smaller tasks so the job isn't so overwhelming that they don't even know where to start. You are the one who is functioning in that capacity as a leader in your home in that area.

The husband is always to be the leader and the priest of the home, but there is an extremely important leadership position that women also have in the home. We must all take our leadership positions in the home seriously. You designate areas of responsibility, you lay things out so your children know what needs to be done, you teach them what is expected of them and you show them how they will see the benefits when they follow a plan of action.

Children learn to feel good about themselves when they accomplish something worthwhile. Even at a very young age, they see that when they've finished a job they can be proud. They can know they've pleased you because they did what you asked them to do.

A sense of unity is created because they are working with every other family member to accomplish what needs to be done. Having a plan and being specific helps remove the opportunity for confusion, jealousy or strife to enter into their lives. You are teaching them how to accomplish what God is going to put in their lives later. When young children learn how to organize and plan in the smaller things of life, then when God begins to speak to them about His plan for them in the bigger things of life, they will know how to organize and plan in order to see it come to pass.

SIGNIFICANCE

The local church works the same way. We can accomplish all that God desires for us to accomplish when we're in our places doing what we're called to do. We must be instrumental in seeing to it that every person knows that his or her part is important. We don't want anyone feeling he or she is left out. No one is insignificant. That would be a missing piece of the puzzle.

Even your job is a place where you can see the principle of planning and leadership work effectively. Sometimes you go to work on Monday morning and think, "How in the world am I going to get all this stuff done?" Or, maybe it's Friday, and you say, " I can't believe it's the end of the week. Where did all the time go?"

Develop a plan of action as a leader. Write things down. Prioritize your list. When your thoughts are organized, you're more prepared to conquer your week. You can eliminate being frustrated on Friday afternoon because nothing has gotten done.

Nehemiah succeeded because, as a leader, he was able to succeed far beyond his own ability through teamwork. He set the stage so that God could work through all His people. He ensured that they were not overwhelmed or unable to complete what he told them to do. **The keys were organization, cooperation and unity**. Guidelines and boundaries were set for each of them.

Leadership

We all know that we need those boundaries and guidelines. When we're within our boundaries and guidelines, there is a sense of peace, security and confidence created in us.

As part of these boundaries and guidelines, attitude becomes a key ingredient in the way we work and lead. I'm sure not all of the people of Jerusalem maintained a correct attitude at all times. In fact, I'm pretty sure that there were some skirmishes. Nehemiah may have had to correct people from time to time.

Overall, judging by the success, I believe the children of Israel saw that the hand of God was in their project and were able to keep the goal in front of them. That's the key to leadership. Everyone who is involved must always know for whom they are working.

For whom are you working? This can be very simple in every situation. You are always working for Jesus. This fact alone lets you know what you want to accomplish. When you know for whom you are working, you have a better idea of what you have to accomplish. Then you can see that your part is vital. Then your attitude will remain correct. This knowledge is the beginning of wise leadership .

VICTORY

As the wall project was completed, everyone recognized that God had done a great work. The Children of Israel, with Nehemiah's unfailing leadership, had won a victory.

SUCCESS QUESTIONS

(1) Nehemiah understood the problem, the solution and the urgency involved in rebuilding the wall around Jerusalem. In one area of your life, describe a problem, then outline the solution and discuss the urgency in solving that problem.

(2) In the above problem, how can you involve a team in the solution?

(3) What additional ways can better planning help in solving the problem and maximizing your team's efforts?

Chapter Six

Faith

> *But it came to pass, that when Sanballat heard that we builded the walls, he was wroth, and took great indignation and mocked the Jews.*
>
> *And he spake before his brethren and the army of Samaria, and said, What do these feeble Jews? will they fortify themselves? will they sacrifice? will they make an end in a day? will they revive the stones out of the heaps of the rubbish which are burned?*
>
> *Now Tobiah the Ammonite was by him, and he said, Even that which they build, if a fox go up, he shall even break down their stone wall.*
> (Nehemiah 4:1-3)

ALWAYS THE CRITIC

Now where have we heard from these two guys before? Remember in Chapter 2 how Sanballat and Tobiah mocked and ridiculed the people and the plan. They're ba-a-a-ck! They show up to taunt the workers who are rebuilding the wall.

Can you get a picture of this in your mind? The workers are tired from day after day of work. They have done foundation work, but they haven't seen a lot of progress in what they're doing. They've been working diligently, but there is still much to be done. All of a sudden, these two men show up again and begin to tease and taunt them. Then, according to verse 8, the scorners were threatening to fight and hinder the project.

What would you do if this happened? Would you be tempted to quit and go home?

The children of Israel reacted with faith-filled words: *Hear, O our God; for we are despised: and turn their reproach upon their own head, and give them for a prey in the land of captivity. Nevertheless we made our prayer unto our God, and set a watch against them day and night, because of them. (Nehemiah 4:4, 9)*

Prayer is always the proper response to any situation. Once again, the workers quickly called out to God in prayer. The purpose of the taunting and ridicule was to cause the laborers to be discouraged and to stop their work. But Nehemiah rallied the people together and began to pray and seek the face of God.

These people kept building, for the people had a mind to work. They understood faith. They bought into the big picture. They firmly established in their minds that they were going to do what God had told them to do.

We must have a mind to work! When the opposition of the enemy comes against us, and when we begin to step out in faith to do what God has called us to do, we must also have a mind to work. We must have great determination—nothing worthwhile is ever accomplished without it. If we don't have resolute faith, any opposition aimed at us will cause us to stop working.

OPPOSITION

There are different degrees of opposition that you and I will face in our lives. Sometimes we'll just shrug it off and continue to do what we're called to do. But sometimes the opposition is very strong. The enemy will use whatever he can to bring destruction into our lives. He loves to cause us to cease walking with God, working for God or ministering for God. The enemy will use every opposition and every opportunity he can to cause us to stop.

When we sense that he is pressing against us, that's the time when we need to rise up in faith. We need to pray and seek God. We need to trust God as we press through the opposition. Once you've done it one time, you'll see that it is possible to do it every time. No matter how difficult the opposition against us, God can help us overcome it.

PRAISE THE LORD AND PASS THE SWORDS

In reading Verse 15 of Chapter 4, we can see that the people did what they needed to do in the spirit. They began to pray, and seek the face of God. They rebuked the evil, scorning powers. They incorporated the power of God into their work.

But they also did something that was very natural. God wants to use our natural ability and this is the evidence.

Faith

And it came to pass, when our enemies heard that it was known unto us, and God had brought their council to nought, that we returned all of us to the wall, every one unto this work.

And it came to pass from that time forth, that the half of my servants wrought in the work, and the other half of them held both the spears, the shields, and the bows, and the habergeons (swords); and the rulers were behind all the house of Judah.

They which builded on the wall, and they that bare burdens, with those that laded, every one with one of his hands wrought in the work, and with the other hand held a weapon. For the builders, every one had his sword girded by his side, and so builded. And he that sounded the trumpet was by me. And I said unto the nobles, and to the rulers, and to the rest of the people, The work is great and large, and we are separated upon the wall, one far from another.

In what place therefore ye hear the sound of the trumpet, resort you thither unto us: our God shall fight for us.

So we labored in the work: and half of them held the spears from the rising of the morning till the stars appeared.

Likewise at the same time said I unto the people, Let every one with the servant lodge within Jerusalem, that in the night they may be a guard to us, and labour on the day.

So neither I, nor my brethren, nor my servants, nor the men of the guard which followed me, none of us put off our clothes, saving that every one put them off for washing.

 (Nehemiah 4:15-23**)**

In other words, Nehemiah initiated a practical plan to keep the project going forward, no matter what the enemy sought to do. While half of the people worked, the other half guarded and protected the people and the wall.

The workers who were rebuilding the walls needed a plan. They needed to guard and protect themselves so that their enemies couldn't come in and bring destruction to what they had already done. So while one group held the sword, the other group worked.

I believe that they traded jobs back and forth. One day a man might serve as a guard, and the next day he did manual labor. This protected their physical bodies from overwork by providing a time of rest. They were prepared for battle if the need arose. At the same time the work continued.

Even in the face of fierce opposition, they kept building the walls. Even when they were being mocked and ridiculed and taunted, they built the walls. Even when they knew that there might be an attack against their lives, they built the walls. That needs to be the position we take in our lives.

SUCCESS

God has given us everything we need to build, to work and to establish the kingdom of God in every area of our lives. We need to see that we are able because God is able. No task is too large. We already have what it takes to work and accomplish the will of God in our lives.

Beyond that, when the body of Christ functions together as a unit, watch out! When we work together, pray together and build together, we can do absolutely miraculous things. Like the workers on the wall, we must be the ones who stand guard against the attack of the enemy that would come against others while they are working.

SUCCESS QUESTIONS

(1) As you begin to succeed beyond your abilities, what differences would you like to see in your life? In your family's lives? In the lives of those around you?

(2) How can you become a better "guard" to help those around you who are working for Christ?

(3) What "walls" need rebuilding around you? How can you begin rebuilding them?

Chapter Seven

Unity

$\mathcal{U}$ntil now, the conflicts faced by the cupbearer and his wall-builders were external ones. One by one, Nehemiah and his team overcame each obstacle. Then we read in Chapter 5 verse 1: *And there was a great cry of the people and of their wives against their brethren the Jews.*

In short order, an internal conflict emerges. Why should we be surprised? Just before the greatest victories often comes the worst attacks—often from those closest to us.

CONFLICTS

Usually, internal strife can be more severe than when the enemy tries to strike from outside. Attacks from within are usually devastating because they are happening with and to people who are supposed to be working with you in unity.

Nehemiah found himself face to face with this heartbreaking situation. It was serious. But, Nehemiah knew how to respond because he was continually seeking God. By now his dependence upon God was well documented. I believe he was always talking to God. When he needed help, he would go immediately to God with his need.
What a powerful testimony. The Bible tells us if we lack wisdom, then we need to ask God and He will liberally supply wisdom to us. That's what Nehemiah did. God reciprocated and supplied his servant with wisdom to deal with every one of the problems that he encountered. In Chapter 5, Nehemiah needed extraordinary wisdom to handle one of the great chal-

lenges that always seems to enter the picture anytime God's people attempt to do anything together—internal strife.

DISSENSION

Fatigued with hard labor and harassed from their enemies, some of the wall-builders reached a breaking point. Remember, these were people who had returned to their homeland with wonderful visions of greatness and plenty. What they found was destroyed buildings, broken-down walls and enemies who were ever present to overrun them again.

Some had been pushed to the point of borrowing money and mortgaging their lands or houses to pay for food and the excise taxes to the Persian government. From what we read in Chapter 5, it was apparent that some families even had to sell their children as slaves.

Nehemiah found himself in a place where he had to rebuke his own people because they were using and taking advantage of each other:

> *And I was very angry when I heard their cry and these words. Also I said, It is not good that ye do: ought ye not to walk in the fear of our God because of the reproach of the heathen our enemies? ...I pray you, let us leave off this usury.*
> *Restore, I pray you, to them, even this day, their lands, their vineyards, their oliveyards, and their houses, also the hundredth part of the money, and of the corn, the wine, and the oil, that ye exact of them.*

They said they, We will restore them, and will require nothing of them; so will we do as thou sayest... (Nehemiah 5: 6, 9, 10-12)

Nehemiah took control of the situation, rebuked the people who were abusing each other and the usurers repented. A cursory look at history and even an elementary knowledge of human nature should let you know how awesome a miracle this result was!

That miracle birthed more miracles. Restoration brings back a spirit of unity. It brings back the ability to work for and with God. It brings back the power to stand in strength. It gives an added ability to defeat the enemy.

I can't help but imagine that if the people had not repented and changed their ways, the outcome of this whole undertaking would have turned out very differently.

You see, when restoration comes, the ability to move forward in God also returns. We need always look for restoration in every problem. We can't be content to just sit back and say, "Oh well. This too shall pass. It will end before too long. Surely it will go away." We must find our plan of attack through prayer, pursue that plan and look for the path of restoration.

It doesn't matter what problem we may be facing. It might be sickness, disease or finances. It might be a lack of unity in your family, or it might be an emotional distress in your own mind. Regardless of what problems you might be facing, God always has a path of restoration. The Bible says that the path of the righteous burns brighter and brighter. So if we choose to walk down the path where God has called us to walk, then our path will become more and more powerful as restoration comes. While we're waiting for the restoration, we've just got to keep walking in unity. Why should we stop doing what God has called us to do just because someone else might not be walking in unity with us at the moment?

There is an anointing and a power that rests upon us when we choose the path of unity. The Bible says how good and pleasant it is for men and brethren to dwell together in unity. We need to seek that place in our lives, regardless of the circumstances. We can remove all fear, doubt and discouragement by putting the Word of God to work in our lives.

WISDOM

I believe God gave Nehemiah wise counsel on how to stand against the attack of the enemy during that time of building and restoration. The Bible says that a wise man is strong and a man of understanding increases in strength and as a leader. He was succeeding far beyond his own abilities. He was increasing in new levels of authority over the people. They were willing to hear what he said. They were willing to follow him, even in the midst of internal conflict. When he confronted the people, they responded: *We will restore them, and will require nothing of them; so will we do as thou sayest. (Nehemiah 5:12)*

They responded favorably. Even at a time when some were doing the wrong thing by profiting from suffering, the children of Israel were overwhelmingly willing to make things right by doing what Nehemiah asked them to do. His strength as a leader kept increasing because he was continually increasing in the wisdom of God.

INSIGHT FROM GOD

No matter where you and I function in our God-ordained leadership capacity—at home, church or at your job—our leadership skills increase by the wisdom of God. We must never leave the wisdom of God out of any area of our lives.

Nehemiah was continually growing in that wisdom. He always seemed to have the correct answer to the problem. He always knew how to instruct the people for victory. Every time there was a need, God gave him the solution. By his wisdom, Nehemiah always knew the correct answer for the problem that was at hand.

Don't you want life to work that way for you? It can! By seeking God's wisdom, we can always have the correct answer for every problem that we face. It doesn't happen through our own knowledge or our own ability, but it's by the wisdom of God. Because Nehemiah continually sought the face and wisdom of God, he always had the correct answer.

God's way is perfect. When we rely on the perfection of God, then we can also see perfection happen in our lives. We can then function in the leadership capacity to which God has called us.

SUCCESS QUESTIONS

(1) Different challenges bring different reactions. Why were the incidents in Chapter 5 so important that Nehemiah had to stop the work and address the issues?

(2) What do we learn from Nehemiah from this chapter?

(3) How can Nehemiah's wise reaction help you in your tough projects?

Chapter Eight

Finishing

Succeeding beyond your Ability

The work was almost complete. Nehemiah had almost finished what God put on his heart to do. He had seen miracle after miracle. He had prayed, found favor, faced the opposition, stopped internal strife, done the work by building his team and now he was almost done.

COMPLETION

You know how you feel when you're almost at the end of a long project? You rejoice and you're happy because you're anticipating the end result. I believe that's how Nehemiah felt. He had diligently sought God, and he had seen God move in a mighty way. He had prayed and overcome all the attacks and obstacles that stood in his way. For a cupbearer from Persia, he had come a long way—literally, figuratively and spiritually.

We've looked at the leadership qualities in his life. He handled every situation that came against him in a way that produced the results that God desired. Now, the work is almost completed. They had all worked together. Nehemiah had organized and planned the work. The people had cooperated and flowed in unity. They had accomplished great things. So it's not hard to imagine at this point that Nehemiah was reflecting back over everything that had happened and thought, "I'm almost there. All that's left to be finished is putting the doors on the gates. That's all that's left and then the City of Jerusalem will be secure again.

It will be the place of refuge and strength for His people God intended it to be. I know we are home free now. Nothing else could possibly happen because there's only one thing left to do.

Nehemiah deserved to be able to relax and enjoy his victory, don't you think?

We ought to be able to relax and enjoy our victories, too. However, the devil doesn't work that way. The Bible says that he is like a roaring lion, seeking whom he may devour. Since he's continually seeking to destroy our lives, he knows that we are particularly vulnerable near the end of a major project. That's what he thought of Nehemiah.

The cupbearer is at a place where he should be able to relax and enjoy his victory. All of a sudden, though, he's faced with a new challenge.

Like a B-grade movie, the bad guys arrive on the scene again—Sanballat and Tobiah. These were the same men Nehemiah had dealt with over and over again. They came back to cause more problems. You'd think that they would have learned. How many times does the devil have to be defeated before he learns that he can't mess with you? Well, these men hadn't learned their lesson yet.

When they learned that the wall had been built and the project was almost completed, they decided to put another obstacle in Nehemiah's path to keep him from completing the work.

Succeeding beyond your Ability

BY INVITATION ONLY

As recorded in Chapter 6:2, Sanballat and Tobiah formulated a cunning plan against Nehemiah. They extended an invitation to him to meet with them in one of the villages in the plain of Ono. Their intent was to draw him out and destroy him. Nehemiah, as usual, was prayed up and on top of things. He was not at all fooled by their enticement. He immediately recognized what they were trying to do. According to verses 3-4, Nehemiah sent a pointed message: *And I sent messengers unto them, saying, I am doing a great work so that I cannot come down: why should the work cease, whilst I leave it, and come down to you? Yet they sent unto him four times after this sort; and I answered them after the same manner.*

Four times the enticers asked Nehemiah to come and meet with them, but each time his reply was the same: "No, way! Why should I stop the great work of God that I'm doing here to come down to meet with you?" I looked at a map to see where the plain of Ono was, and discovered that it was quite a distance from Jerusalem. These men were trying their best to separate Nehemiah from the place God had called him.

SEPARATION

How often do we find that happening in our own lives? Separation from the plan of God and from the move of God is still a tactic that the enemy uses today in our lives. If he can separate us from what God has called us to do, from the people He's called us to be with and from the place where

He's called us to be—then Satan has free reign in our lives. There are many reasons why separation comes, and many ways that it manifests itself.

People often times leave the church because they get offended. They make a choice to separate themselves, based on the lies of the enemy. They allow themselves to be separated from the place that God has ordained them to be because of some offense. If they would only stop and look at the circumstances, so many times they'd see that it was really over something trivial and insignificant. Instead, they allow the enemy to come in and separate them from the place that God's called them to.

Another way separation comes is through a lack of knowledge. If we don't know what God has called us to do, where He's called us to be, or if we don't know the Word the way that we need to, then we can get separated from the plan of God for our lives.

A third way of separation is through deception (the lies of the enemy). We must be wise when it comes to the tactics of the enemy. We cannot allow ourselves to remain ignorant concerning the ways the devil tries to bring hindrances into our lives. We have to realize that deception and lies can come through other people. We can see it plainly in the life of Nehemiah. These men were trying to kill him! And, they were prepared to use any lie or deception in the book to do it. We have to be able to see the many ways the enemy will try to deceive us. It may be through very well-meaning people. It may be through circumstances—things that sound right, look right and feel right, but aren't right. The Bible says that we should have our senses exercised to discern between good and evil. In other words, we must be able to tell what is right and what is wrong. God does not want us to be a people who become deceived and move away from His plan for us.

We can become separated because of **fear**. Fear will always distract us from the move of God and from the call of God on our lives. Many times we can't do what God has called us to do because we're afraid we're going to fail. Fear and deception work together. The enemy will even use the Word of God against the people of God. Think about the Garden of Eden. The devil twisted the Word of God around in such a way that he made Eve fearful that God was holding out on her, that the Lord wasn't going to give her everything she desired. Satan deceived her into believing a lie. The result: separation from God.

Twisted thinking often results in fear. Fear and faith can never work together. Instead, they work against each other. If we are walking in fear, then the faith of God can't work in us. That fear can very easily separate us from God. How can we walk with God if we're not trusting in him?

A blessing that becomes a curse can separate us from God. There have been so many times in our years of ministry that we've prayed with men and women for a job, for a mate, or for something good that God desires to see come to pass in their lives. Then, as soon as the answer comes, we never see those people again inside the four walls of the church.

They actually allow a blessing from God to become a means of separation from the plan of God for their lives. They get a piece of the puzzle, but they leave before the beautiful picture is complete.

NEW TACTICS

As mentioned, four different times the enemy tried to get Nehemiah to walk away from the plan of God, and four times he refused them. Finally, his enemies changed their scheme.

We must never become complacent when it comes to our enemy. Just because something he throws at us doesn't work, that doesn't mean he's not going to try something else. In verse 5 of Chapter 6 relates, *Then sent Sanballat his servant unto me in like manner the fifth time with an open letter in his hand.*

Nehemiah received a letter with an indication that it was not necessarily for him personally, but was to be read aloud to everyone. The letter accused the Jews of planning a rebellion, and it accused them of intending to make Nehemiah their king. They lied about the reason why Nehemiah was restoring the city of Jerusalem and the walls. And they accused him of setting himself up in a position to become their king.

We read in verse 9: *For they all made us afraid, saying, Their hands shall be weakened from the work, that it be not done. Now therefore, O God, strengthen my hands.*

We see Nehemiah acknowledging the fact that he was beginning to be a little bit fearful. He was afraid that his hands would become weak and he wouldn't be able to finish the task. So he prayed to God to strengthen his hands. I believe this type of prayer was effective for Nehemiah because it wasn't the only type of prayer that he incorporated into his life.

God doesn't want every prayer we pray to be, "Oh, God! Please help me!" God desires that we have a life-style of prayer. He wants us to be committed to Him, surrendered to Him and acknowledging Him as our source of strength and power. If we do that continually and trust in God as our strength, then when we get in a tough spot, we can say, "God, strengthen my hands." It's one of those quick calls to God that He hears, but He doesn't want that to be the only type of prayer that He hears from us.

Notice that even when fear arose in Nehemiah, he didn't go crazy. He didn't start doing weird and goofy things. He remained calm and in control.

So many times when the enemy puts pressure on us, we just go bonkers. We start doing things that we would never do under normal circumstances. We can do such silly things that we get out of the place that God has called us to be in. But Nehemiah didn't do that. He remained constant. Sometimes it doesn't even take prayer. It just takes a little bit of rational thought for us to recognize the strategy of the enemy.

DANGER

We see in Verse 10 that a man named Shemaiah urges the cupbearer to go inside the temple and shut the doors. He told Nehemiah that his enemies were coming to kill him. But, Nehemiah again saw the deception. He knew that God had not sent this messenger to him. Sure enough, he later found out that Tobiah and Sanballat had hired the man to trick him. The only way Nehemiah could have perceived those things was by the wisdom of God working in him. And the wisdom of God could only be working in him if he was continuing to seek the counsel of God.

These guys kept throwing some pretty big punches at Nehemiah, but he didn't fall for any of them. Even when they tried on four different occasions to get him to come and meet with them, he refused them every time. Sometimes we think that if we hear the same thing more than once, it must be God. Our enemy is not going to give up just because we don't fall for a lie the first time.

Even though Nehemiah kept hearing the same thing, he knew what he was doing was right. He definitely had the courage of his convictions. How many of us, if we were in Nehemiah's shoes, might have been tempted to say, "Well, you know, all I have left to do are the doors. I've worked really hard for a long time, so maybe I'll just take some time to relax and go and see what they want. Maybe they've changed. Maybe they don't really mean me any harm. I don't have that much left to do, and I can get somebody else to finish that. I really need a break."

But Nehemiah said, "No. I've been called by God to be here. God has made a way for me to do this work. He has opened doors for me. He sent me with letters from the king. He has provided for me. He kept me all the way on my journey. He has kept us safe from every attack. He has given me wisdom against the tactics of the enemy. I'm not going to stop. God has called me to do this and I'm going to do it. It's not complete yet, and I won't stop until the wall is finished!"

FINISHING

God wants to see "finish line" faith and perseverance in every one of us. It doesn't matter if we're close to the goal or whether we've just begun. It doesn't matter how large or small the task. We need to be diligent. We've got to determine that we will not stop until the task is complete.

With children, we must refuse to stop until we've accomplished everything God has put in our hearts to do. In marriages, we must refuse to stop until we have overcome every obstacle that divides couples. In any area of ministry, we must refuse to stop until every desire of our hearts has been fulfilled.

Understandably, there are some areas that require more perseverance than others. Whatever the case, we have to determine in our hearts that we will not stop. Perseverance requires diligence, strength and prayer. Thankfully, we have all of those at our disposal. God is a God who never grows weary or loses His strength. He wants to see us successfully complete the work that He's called us to do. He never sets us up for failure, only for victory. We must not allow anything the enemy is doing to separate us from the call of God.

If we find ourselves separated, all we have to do is ask God for restoration. As we are diligent to do what God has called us to do, and as we determine in our hearts to see the finished work, He will strengthen our hands and cause us to succeed in everything He has called us to do.

HEART

When we find ourselves in a place in our lives where we feel we just can't handle one more attack from the enemy, we can take heart! God never grows weary and He never loses His power. He will strengthen us for the battle. We remember that the battle is not ours, but it's the Lord's. He never gets tired and He never quits.

I wonder if that's where Nehemiah was? Surely he must have thought, "Why don't these guys just go home and leave me alone? Why do they continue to make trouble for me? What did I do to deserve this?" When we grow weary in the battle and just need to rest, then we need to just rest in God. He's our rest. He's our strength. He's the one giving us the power. And, He's the one who fights the battle for us. We must never try to do it by ourselves. When we do that, we'll lose every time. But, if we put on the whole armor of God and let God do the rest, we'll be victorious every time.

SUCCESS QUESTIONS

(1) How have you overcome Satan's attacks recently?

(2) How could you have used Nehemiah's example to handle those attacks differently?

(3) What does success mean to you?

(4) How has your concept of success changed during this study of Nehemiah?

Conclusion

Success

SETTING THE GATES

So the wall was finished in the twenty and fifth day of the month Elul, in fifty and two days. And it came to pass, that when all our enemies heard thereof, and all the heathen that were about us saw these things, they were much cast down in their own eyes: for they perceived that this work was wrought of our God.
(Nehemiah 6:15-16)

One final attack came before the walls were completed. His enemies knew that if the gates were not set properly, they could still get in. The strength of the city would be compromised. But Nehemiah stood firm and the walls were completed.

How many times in our lives do we find that it's that one last attack that gets us to stop? How often do we fail just before the finish line? How many times have we grown weary near the point of our victory, and then we stop because the enemy rallies his troops for one final attack?

Perhaps you've been seduced to think, "Man, I'm home free. I've defeated the devil. Jesus defeated the devil, and I've stood on the authority He has given me. The devil can't bother me anymore." Then as we gloat over the near-victory, the rest of our enemies show up.

There is one sure-fire way that the last attack cannot destroy our mission. There is a plan we can follow to ensure that attack won't be successful. Ephesians 6:10-13 gives this winning strategy:

> *Finally, my brethren, be strong in the Lord, and in the power of his might.*
>
> *Put on the whole armour of God, that ye may be able to stand against the wiles of the devil.*
>
> *For we wrestle not against flesh and blood, but against principalities, against powers, against the rulers of the darkness of this world, against spiritual wickedness in high places.*
>
> *Wherefore take unto you the whole armor of God that you may be able to withstand in the evil day, and having done all, to stand.*

The verses in Ephesians 6 tells us, specifically, how each piece of our armor should empower us:

- Our loins are girded about with truth.
- We put on the breastplate of righteousness.
- Our feet are shod with the preparation of the gospel of peace.
- We take up the shield of faith, which enables us to quench all the fiery darts of our enemies.
- We put on the helmet of salvation.
- We wield the sword of the spirit which is the Word of God.
- We pray always with all types of prayer.

Succeeding beyond your Ability

Many times we go out the front lines of the battle unarmed. We think that because we put on the armor of God yesterday, we're still ready for the battle. Like Nehemiah, as we are commanded in Ephesians 6, we must be more diligent in our preparation for battle. It's just like getting dressed every day. You don't stand around undressed today just because you got dressed yesterday. We wouldn't even think about not getting dressed today.

It needs to be the same way in the spirit, especially when we can see an attack against our lives. We must always be prepared for battle. Preparation obviously doesn't mean going down to the store and investing in a natural suit of armor. We're not wrestling against flesh and blood. The battle we're fighting is not in the natural realm; it's in the spiritual realm. It is a spiritual battle. We must be diligent to put on the armor of God.

If you don't cover all the areas, then you're not completely clothed for battle. You are not as prepared in the spirit to fight against the attacks of the enemy as you should be. If you go off to work without putting on your shoes, you are highly vulnerable in a tender area. Your everyday armor is not complete. Certainly, in the spirit realm you cannot afford to leave any part undone.

Nehemiah understood this principle as the children of Israel rebuilt the wall. If he didn't get the gates up, then there was still an opening for the enemy to get in.

WEAK SPOTS

Wherever there is an opening—an area not covered in prayer—the enemy will find that weak spot in the armor and launch his attack there. By praying, we can ensure that we're prepared for what we may face in the spirit. By taking care of our physical bodies, we can ensure our success in the natural. We must be strong in the Lord and in the power of His might.

Never lose sight of the fact that the battle is not ours; it is God's opportunity for victory. He wants to use us in the battle. We're His soldiers. We read in Isaiah 40:28,30:

> *Hast thou not known? hast thou not heard, that the everlasting God, the Lord, the Creator of the ends of the earth, fainteth not, neither is weary. There is no searching of his understanding.*
>
> *But they that wait upon the Lord shall renew their strength; they shall mount up with wings as eagles; they shall run, and not be weary; and they shall walk, and not faint.*

VICTORY

As the wall project was completed, everyone recognized that God had done a great work. The children of Israel, with Nehemiah's unfailing leadership, had won a victory.

Isn't it amazing that when it is definitely settled that a thing can't be done, someone goes out and does it?

As the wall project was completed, everyone recognized that God had done a great work. The children of Israel, with Nehemiah's unfailing leadership, had won a victory.

Isn't it amazing that when it is definitely settled that a thing can't be done, someone goes out and does it?

God blessed the people of Jerusalem, and at the celebration that followed, Ezra began reading from the book of the Law. Six hours later, he was still reading. Then, according to Chapter 8, the nation began waking up to the fact that God had done something historic and life-changing. Before, they were in the midst of a tedius rebuilding project. Now, as they stepped back and saw what they had helped create, the people began realizing how marvelous and wonderful the project really was.

Suddenly, a revival broke out: *And Ezra blessed the Lord, the great God. And all the people answered, Amen, Amen, with lifting up their hands: and they bowed their heads, and worshipped the Lord with their faces to the ground. (Nehemiah 8:6)*

How do we know a true revival was sweeping over the people? The people wept. They were changed. They rejoiced. They found a new understanding of the Word of God. And life in Jerusalem would never be the same because the people knew God had done a great work—naturally and spiritually. That, by definition, is revival!

NEHEMIAH'S LEGACY

He was a captive cupbearer in King Artaxerxes Persian court, but he listened when God called him to a higher calling. He learned that God's vision and calling brings faith, which knows no boundaries. More importantly, he discovered that the end of a God-inspired victory is God Himself!

We don't know a lot about what happened to Nehemiah after the wall was rebuilt. We do know that Nehemiah stayed in Jerusalem for a dozen years, during which the children of Israel seemed to live well. He did return to Persia and the service of the king. How long he stayed in Susa is not recorded, but eventually he asked King Artaxerxes for permission to return to his homeland (13:6).

When he returned to Jerusalem, he was once again used as a bold leader to bring his countrymen to a new level of repentance and revival. And when his work was completed, Nehemiah ended his ministry with these words: *Remember me, O my God, for good. (Nehemiah 13:31)*

Even in the end, he desired favor from the Lord to fulfill his calling.

YOUR CALLING

What are you called to do? What visions have been placed in your heart by the Lord?

As Nehemiah understood, you have much to do. God has given you great opportunities and open doors. The Lord has given you talents, skills and dreams that are unique to you.

What will you do with these wonderful gifts?

To succeed beyond your ability, you must go beyond visions and dreams. You must finish what God gives you to do. You must be willing to go through the process of brokenness, prayer, preparation, leadership, faith and building unity. You will be required to take risks. You will be called to sacrifice your personal goals for bigger visions. Like Nehemiah, you will face scorn and criticism. But in the end, if you keep going, you will see victory in ways that relatively few people get to experience.

You can do it! You can succeed beyond your ability. You can cross the finish line. You can rebuild many walls. You are just one person, but you can make a difference. You can impact your world.

Nehemiah did. You can, too!

SUCCESS QUESTIONS

(1) What area of your life most resembles Nehemiah?
(2) What victories have you celebrated recently?
(3) What great victories would you like to see?
(4) What one thing holds you back from reaching new levels of success?
(5) What are you willing to do in order to overcome that major hindrance?